MW00489101

ALMANAC OF QUIET DAYS

(Poems)

Lois Parker Edstrom

Photographs by Emily Gibson

Copyright© Lois Parker Edstrom
ISBN: 978-93-90601-98-1

First Edition: 2021
Rs. 200/-

Cyberwit.net
HIG 45 Kaushambi Kunj, Kalindipuram
Allahabad - 211011 (U.P.) India
http://www.cyberwit.net
Tel: +(91) 9415091004
E-mail: info@cyberwit.net

No part of this book may be reproduced or transmitted in any form or by any means, electronic, mechanical, photocopying, or otherwise, without the express written consent of Lois Parker Edstrom.

Printed at Thomson Press India Limited.

Dear Louise,

May you be blessed by this !

In memory of my mother
Grace Putnam Parker

Emily Gibson dedicates her photographs to:
"the Creator of all things bright and beautiful,
who inspires words of wisdom and wonder."

Emily Gibson

CONTENTS

Nature's Hush   9

Ripening Season   11

Road Trip   13

An Invitation   15

Harvest Bee   17

Silhouette   19

Cathedral of Light   21

The Enchanted Forest   23

Narnia   25

Mysterious Mycelium   27

There Among Thorns   29

Fences   31

Fresh Air   33

Truth of Purpose   35

The Sum of Their Work   37

Perfectionism   39

Bookworm   41

Fragile Beauty   43

Red Sun Red Moon   45

Motif of Grief   47

Shades of Loneliness   49

Tree House   51

Mount Shuksan   53

Winter Art   55

Snow Geese   57

Gathering Sweetness   59

Smitten   61

Council to a Teenager   63

Grasshopper as Art   65

On the Altar of Summer   67

Dream Boy   69

A Curious Knowing   71

Autumn Gold   73

The Beauty of Difference   75

Getting Along   77

Homer   79

Out of the Blue   81

Innovation   83

Art in the Hen House   85

Pitchfork Grace   87

Porcine Dreams   89

An Evening Walk   91

Like a Bad Habit   93

Poets and Rodents   95

Ode to Old Age   97

One Room   99

Peaceful Valley   101

The Far Edge of Longing   103

Swarm   105

Handout   107

Acknowledgments   108

You don't take a photograph.
You ask quietly to borrow it.
Unknown

NATURE'S HUSH

Something has quieted the poet's voice.
Something on the edge of mystery.

Is dawn rising in the mists of morning?
Has the first frost of autumn cooled the air?

Maples gleam in harmony with the season;
how easily they release what is no longer needed.

In the bounty of pasture two Haflingers graze,
the contented comfort of togetherness.

How to settle into serenity such as this?
Ask the silence. Ask the light.

RIPENING SEASON

Seed heads will begin to nod or bow on the stem
when they are ready to harvest.

Ancient grains that nourish and sustain show
us when they are ripe. Oh, that we could come
to our own maturity with such assurance.

False starts, wrong turns, trials, pain, pinches
of regret. Lessons of patience and humility?

I think of this as we travel through the Palouse,
the fine golden shine of wheat and barley fields
spread in undulating slopes and knolls to the horizon.

Under persistent urging of sunlight,
the grain grows and ripens, giving itself
to harvest and the eventual warmth
of a baker's hands. Then, kneading,
stretching, lightness, and rising.

ROAD TRIP

The poem travels and no one knows
where it's going. It tours scenic
byways, roaming in and around hills
and valleys, searching for pockets of truth.

Soon enough the poem encounters a blind
corner, a steep upgrade, a sheer drop-off.
It trembles and is jolted by unexpected
bumps and potholes.

Like a young person, the poem must journey
alone: a stage of separation to test and explore
and eventually return to where it began.

With time it travels the backroads of memory,
an arduous passage, rich with promise
and risk.

Along the way it basks in the early morning
gleam of a wheat field, the silver shine of the sea,
and in the silence of a forest finds rest.
As sunlight slants down the trunks of ancient
evergreens, the poem follows the light
and finds its way.

AN INVITATION

Each day comes wrapped in choices
tied with the twine of possibilities.
Tug a frayed edge, your life
tumbles out.

Think of the farmer who trusts
the promise of soil to grow
the wheat, his vision of sturdy
hands that will knead the dough,
shape the loaves, and of the patience
to wait for rising.

Come break a morsel from the loaf.
Dip into the lemon curd and honey.

HARVEST BEE

After college and a few years away,
he came back to the family farm.
For many years he lived the seasons,
accommodating weather, reconciling
himself to the land.

There in the Palouse he tended undulating
fields of wheat, twelve hundred acres
planted and harvested each year.

Winter saw the fields seeded, green shoots
of spring pushing through the soil,
and by summer, wheat nodding and bowing
in honor of its ripeness.

When they heard, they came. Neighbors
nearby and those fifty miles away
climbed into combines and grain trucks
as word spread over the Palouse
that cancer had disabled one of their own.

He watched as sixty farmers orchestrated
the harvest: a composition of precise movements,
a triumph of goodness, bringing in the crop
in six hours, work that would have taken him
three weeks to complete.

SILHOUETTE

It's difficult to tell where water ends
and sky begins. Are those islands
or clouds? And does it matter?

Do we always need a starting point
to define what lies ahead? Could we
move beyond boundaries, open
ourselves to not knowing, into
a leeway of imagination?

In the foreground, brush, stripped
by autumn's initiative, thrusts bare
remains against a limitless prospect—
its own kind of beauty.

CATHEDRAL OF LIGHT

See how sunlight falls
into a forest creating columns
of shadow and slanted brightness?

Light slides down the trunks of silent
evergreens, partners with the wind
to excite quaking aspens.

It does not give itself to everything,
barely touching the cool damp pockets
where moss fronds glisten

and crumbled remains of fallen
cedars molder in a hollow
of aromatic scent.

The forest awakens and the light
unravelling its darkness sends
rays as pure as love.

THE ENCHANTED FOREST

The children found an opening
in the woods and named it
The Enchanted Forest.

Grandpa bent willow branches
to make miniature chairs and table.
A teapot, tiny cups, and flowers.

Imaginations soared beyond
the overhanging trees and when
Grandma slipped a jar of jellybeans

into the dense cool darkness
of the camp, the children were afraid
to partake, certain the candy

had been put there by a conniving witch.

NARNIA

I've wondered what caused the child
to crawl into that wardrobe,
yet it shouldn't be a surprise.

Children love tight hidden spaces
where imaginations are free
to float in hot air balloons, explore
ocean depths, climb mountains, build
castles, or meet a mysterious lion
radiating goodness.

It must have been an enticement
to crawl between those coats:
ermine, fox, mink, and chinchilla fur
gliding over face and arms.

Yes, this is the wardrobe of C.S. Lewis'
childhood—the wardrobe that opened
to an unexpected land of wonder.

Is it curiosity that takes us
beyond the perimeter of ourselves?

MYSTERIOUS MYCELIUM

Mushrooms rise from the duff
of the forest floor, a humble
beginning, and pop up overnight
fully formed.

Mycelium threads spread underground,
covering large portions of earth,
produce rare truffles, or emerge
as toadstools, puffballs, stinkhorns.

Mushrooms arrange in fairy circles,
appear as elves in red caps—
delectable delicacies or deadly
masquerading killers.

As a small girl, hunting the elusive
fungi with my grandmother, we found
crinkly morel mushrooms beneath a ring
of alder trees, gathered them in a basket.

We dredged them in flour, sautéed
them in butter. All these years later
those tender mushrooms are remembered
as one of the best fares I've ever eaten.

THERE AMONG THORNS

For Emily

Forget about the composition, the balance,
the contrast, the textures. If we had nothing
more than color, it would be enough.

Draw near to what feels heart-close,
soul-bound, how you chanced upon
this unexpected vignette captured
at a perfect moment in time.

So often preoccupied by a larger landscape,
we may overlook nature's grace tucked away
in a corner of a meadow.

Were you startled by an unyielding fence post
gripped by thorns? A dark magenta leaf
so complimentary to green, and a filigree
of dewdrops overlaid against a tangle of brambles?

FENCES

Why is it we may see barbs
as we contemplate a new adventure?

Are we afraid of a little pain?
Is what we want worth
a few scratches?

We are on the outside looking in.
If all we see are obstacles, isn't that a way
of wounding ourselves?

This late summer morning, fog softens
the golden seed pods of wild carrots
and fern fronds bend inward.

See beyond, that green valley rimmed
with evergreens? Step inside your dreams.
Think about what may be there
waiting to get out.

A fence offers protection, but is also
a choice between confinement
and freedom.

FRESH AIR

Look closely; you will see
a screen covering the window,
a thin barrier to keep out pesky
winged-things that may contaminate,
bite, or sting.

And don't we all erect barriers
to protect ourselves—a buffer
to temper words or deeds
that hurt and wound,
pegged by thoughtless people?

Open the window. Breathe deeply.
Let fresh air in. Don't put up a screen
so dense it obscures all that is out there—

a restful shaded yard, a circular road
by which to come and go, and beyond,
a bright sunlight meadow.

TRUTH OF PURPOSE

Spiders come into the world
masters of connection:

silk lines, strong yet light,
carried by the wind

from one tree to another or anchored
in the corner of a window.

Careful attention to orbs, geometric
elegance that captures and protects.

They work with the sureness
of knowing: standard bearers

for the dignity and beauty of work.
In the deepest part of who we are,

can we find the truth of our purpose?

THE SUM OF THEIR WORK

Honeybees travel to find work,
dozens of them among the flowers,
humming their satisfied tune;
like fat bankers in pinstripe suits
they collect their payments.

I sit in the garden, watch
their industrious ways,
wonder what they have chosen
as a vessel for their liquid asset,
where is the repository
for their gold.

In one lifetime
can we ever hope
to invest so wisely?

PERFECTIONISM

They aren't perfect.
They don't need to be.

See how light
embellishes the shape

of the pear, overriding
any blemish.

Can't you taste the sweet
flesh, goodness dripping

down your chin? I say,
perfection is boring

and agree with Voltaire:
perfect is the enemy of good.

BOOKWORM

You know who you are.

You are the person who stockpiles stacks of books
on the bedside table and next to your favorite chair.

The person who sacrifices sleep to read
just one more page.

The person who reads the cereal box when
nothing else is available near the breakfast table.

The girl who falls into an uncovered manhole
walking down a busy street while reading.

The objects of your affection may be
as precious as the Book of Kells

or as sappy as an Archie and Jughead
comic book.

It's the words, the words,
that keep zipping by, telegraphing

an urgent message: *What's next?*
What's next?

FRAGILE BEAUTY

It's just a leaf. A damaged leaf at that,
clinging to a filbert tree ravaged by blight.
The leaf turns partially back upon itself,
riddled with holes, the traumatic result
of voracious insect appetites.

Damaged does not accurately describe
this leaf, the color of rich burgundy wine,
deep purple veins that branch to the tips
of its serrated edge. The holes open the leaf
to light and air, forming a filigree of nature,
an exquisite fragile beauty.

It makes me think of our own traumas,
how they open us, raw and hurting, humble us,
soften and expand us to the pain of others
and when we are most vulnerable we hold on,
weakened, but not necessarily damaged.
Perhaps it is then our scars become beautiful
and an inner loveliness shines through.

RED SUN RED MOON

September 12, 2020

Smoke from wild fires covers the island.
Forests ablaze miles and miles away
surrender to flame, release resinous
fumes into the air smothering
the Pacific Northwest.

As islanders we are familiar with fog
that rolls into the strait, a refreshing
cloud of white lather. Now the air
is blurred brown and foghorns,
impervious to the change, sound
their mournful ballad.

After a year of virus and quarantine,
the red sun, the red moon
punch angry fists through
the haze of our bewilderment.

MOTIF OF GRIEF

Mute Swans mate for life. We have
no way of knowing why
the swan is alone, but we know
of widows and widowers who mourn
the loss of a mate—how death empties
the hours, gives rise to longing
for what cannot be.

This solitary swan turns away
from the shore, leaving a coppery sheen
of sunlight, a white trace of sorrow
flowing from her pristine feathers.

Ahead the water is glossed
in emerald luster as she quietly
glides toward uncertain waters.

Those who grieve know
the quiet twist of loneliness,
know how silence
is imbued with questions.

SHADES OF LONELINESS

So many lonely people, longings
intensified by pandemic and quarantine.

The elderly, old beyond their time
owing to isolation.

Single people who yearn for an enduring
bond with another.

Neglected babies who fail to thrive,
due to lack of touch.

And those who live together disconnected
by antipathy or friction.

Do we all long for something beyond
ourselves? Perhaps a night sky intensifies

a sense of loss, of insignificance, or the need
for a simple touch from another's hand.

This moody image draws the eye upward
toward a break in the clouds, and there

a heartening trace of color.

TREE HOUSE

Everyone needs a place of their own.
A place to nurture dreams, evaluate

secrets. Climb upward, pull
the rope-ladder up behind you.

Settle into the sturdy arms
of the black walnut tree.

Listen.
Enter the silence.

Let your thoughts fly
without destination.

The breeze soothes like a gentle
spirit. Rest and find

the matchless part of yourself.

MOUNT SHUKSAN

I go to the mountains where sky
paints the foothills blue,
where cedar, hemlock, and noble fir
lend their hues to the river and sweet air
carries the resinous sent of evergreens
to itself.

Sunlight seeps into the deep darkness
of forest, spilling across the trunks
of massive trees, brightening
the berries of Salal and Oregon grape.

Above the lake, Mount Shuksan
raises its stony snow-clad face
to all that is possible and I am
diminished and expanded
by its presence.

WINTER ART

Winter slices everything down to bare basics.
Clouds darken and sunlight, weak and pale
as the face of fear, slips out between shifting shadows.

Sodden leaves clump along roadsides
and bunch in porch corners. But oh, the sculptural
beauty of bare willow and alder and birch.

Thin branches touch and overlap forming
intricate triangles of light.
What is it that you find beautiful? a friend asks

as I raise my face to the tops of the denuded,
exposed trees that flare against the sky.
I consider how something made vulnerable

exposes its beauty, and the empty spaces—
a latticework of branches—how one must look
through and beyond the obvious to find what is true.

SNOW GEESE

I wish I could show you how a blizzard

   of snow geese rose from furrowed

white-flocked fields, at this very spot,

   and billowed around the steeple

of the Conway Lutheran Church.

They ascended wind currents, swirling

   like satin ribbons, light as bridal veils.

Their black-tipped wings played chromatic

   scales in octaves of sky as they rose higher

     in the silver light of winter,

      an aria soaring beyond

       our earthbound awe.

GATHERING SWEETNESS

Love buzzes around the room.
You can almost hear the swoosh
and sigh. Its light a soft glow
that spreads over books and toys,
flavors before-bedtime snacks,
lingers in the fragrance and vapors
of bath time.

It hovers over and around
the rocking chair, bounces
from note to note of a lullaby,
enters into prayers and between
clasped fingers—a powerful bridge
linking generations.

A time of gathering sweetness,
of blatant adoration.
Impossible to tell
who loves whom the most.

SMITTEN

Matchmaking usually fails.
He doesn't call.
She isn't interested.

Now an introduction,
and suddenly
a rocket explodes
and fireworks
blossom
in the sky.

It happened in a blink.
The matchmaker,
an unexpected arsonist,
lit the match that sparked
an inferno and two people,
who needed each other,
applied accelerant, fanned
flames into a bright blaze
that will be left to burn.

COUNCIL TO A TEENAGER

An adorable granddaughter
in a family of boys.
We bought her a silver bracelet,
year after year adding a charm
to mark events in her life.

Baby slippers, a heart,
a lighthouse, ferry boat,
and sand dollar; a book,
a flute, a ballerina,
the Eiffel Tower.

For her fifteenth birthday
Grandpa picked out a little frog.
Very cute, but of what significance?

When he gave it to her he said,
This is a reminder: Don't be kissing
any toads. They never turn into
charming princes.

GRASSHOPPER AS ART

We may swoon over the artful beauty
of a dandelion seed head,

yet notice the grasshopper, a shiny warrior
of excellent proportions.

It is poised to leap into future adventures
making music on the way.

A hindleg drawn across the frets
of a forewing and we're called

to a concert hall, to the string section
of an orchestra, to the courtship trill

of a cello.

ON THE ALTAR OF SUMMER

Blackberries call us to the edge of the field,
to the fringe of thicket draped
with scarlet rosehips and misty snowberries.

My grandson and I carry tin pails
to the altar of summer and there
in shadowy depths of brambles,

plump berries glisten like dark suns.
A gentle tug and berries fall softly
into our cupped palms.

Nicked by thorns, our arms bleed,
a reminder that sacrifice is fundamental
to reward.

A raven's curved flight signals
a benediction and we set off for home,
stained and expectant, counting

the steps back to the kitchen
and the taste of blackberry pancakes.

DREAM BOY

You dream dreams so grand they fill
the air, leave tracks upon the sand.

Possibilities, like whitecaps that romp
across the cove, press on, and you,

the wave-chaser, who storm-frolics
in moonlight along the shore

take chances, going out to meet the waves,
toes planted to test if you lay claim

or must retreat, those magnificent waves
cresting, breaking at your feet.

A CURIOUS KNOWING

Before markers appear,
there is a time when you pause,
as if you hear a call. Something
has shifted. Is it the air?
A scent? A curious knowing
that comes without facts.
Summer has turned toward fall.

Later autumn will show itself
with undisguised confidence,
wild color, crisp morning light,
and the wind will page through
a catalog of leaves.

AUTUMN GOLD

It is said,
a ladybug
is a symbol
of good luck.

I say,
golden raspberries
in October
prove it.

THE BEAUTY OF DIFFERENCE

The fires of autumn burn brightly,
a familiar conflagration of red, orange,
and gold; a boisterous letting go
of what has become expendable.
You can hear the crunch and crackle,
as the season turns toward change,
trees offering tinder for the flame.

Here in a quiet corner of the meadow,
the surprise of something different.
It seems like a whisper rather than a shout,
contemplation rather than demand,
colors like the nacreous swirl inside
an oyster, or the skim of an oil-glazed puddle.

If we are willing to approach the unexpected
with an open heart, consider the unfamiliar,
it is all there like happy tears, like the charm
and blessing of raindrops.

GETTING ALONG

I can't help but speculate
these ducks have had a spat.
Aren't the ruffled feathers a giveaway?

Sibling rivalry? Political opponents?
Neighborhood disputes?

One has turned its back on the others.
They are divided, split, facing
in opposite directions with a different
point of view.

Judging by appearances, these are
disgruntled players choosing sides
with a dismal chance
of an optimistic outcome.

However, common sense prevails.
These faultless ducks, having fluffed
their feathers, are drying off, airing out,
removing anything that prevents them
from feeling warm again.

HOMER

Something about that nose,
round as a licorice gumdrop
and massively inquiring.

It brings the world to him,
the lowdown on facts
denied to us.

He knows the rabbit
has been in the garden and where
the interloper has traveled.

He knows who has wandered
through the neighborhood and
can sniff out the bad guys.

He would like to get a whiff of you.
He has an inside track and will know
more about you than you can imagine.

But for now, he has other concerns.
*The cat got into my pen and is making me
nervous, so let me out now please.*

OUT OF THE BLUE

Monday was laundry day for the housewives
of that small rural town. You could almost

hear the collective hum of wringer washing
machines flustering a ration of pillowcases

and sheets. Only one choice of bedding then—
white, white, or white, so the women

added *Mrs. Stewart's Bluing,* a dye,
to the tub to make the whites whiter.

This makes sense if you think about
the complementary affair between yellow

and blue. A clothesline wrapped around
a pulley and anchored to a tall pole

sailed the whites, billowing like clouds,
into a (you guessed it) blue sky,

unless rain dampened expectations.

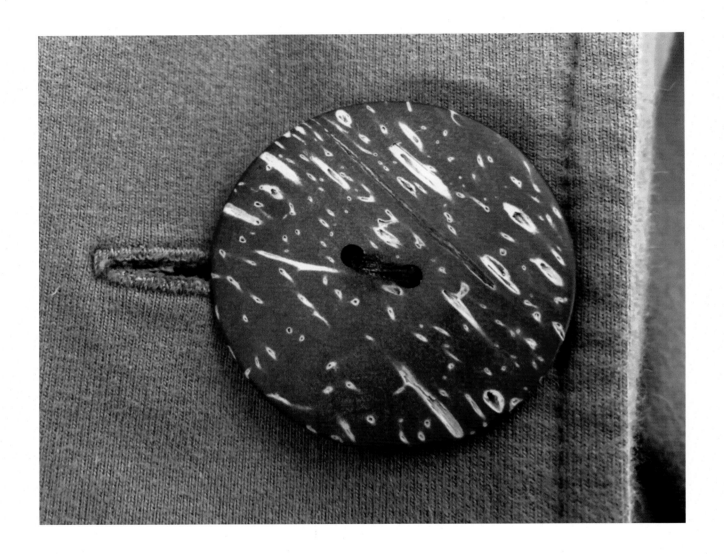

INNOVATION

An ancient object that began
as ornamental: bronze, sterling
and gold buttons displayed
on the clothing of those
who enjoyed prosperity
and privilege.

Ages and ages before someone
thought to design a hole
into which a button would fit.
Amazing how long
it sometimes takes, for us
to figure out how to bring
things together.

ART IN THE HEN HOUSE

No desire to crack this egg.

No need to be nourished
beyond the grace found here.

Follow the curve
of the perfect oval,

the pristine whiteness,
the clean nest of straw.

Simplicity speaks
the language of beauty.

PITCHFORK GRACE

If these boots could talk they'd say,
Let's get it done.

Striding to the barn before dawn,
dew squishing under the soles,
stalls cleaned, horses fed.

Along the wood-chipped path
to the chopping block where axe
divides lengths of alder into firewood.

Up the rise that leads to the pasture,
fences in need of mending, and beyond
to fields of hay lying in windrows
waiting to be baled.

One careful foot after the other
in the cultivated garden, potatoes
unearthed, and on to the orchard,
up rungs of a ladder, golden apples
nestled into baskets.

At day's end, pulled off and left
in a bright kitchen on a braided rug
just inside the door.
Muck, mud, and manure the reward
for a good day of honest work.

PORCINE DREAMS

Do we always want more than we need?
More time off. More travel.

Just one more piece of that tempting dark chocolate
filled with caramel, sprinkled with sea salt.

To hear that you're loved one more time
then again and again.

The best wine, the gourmet dinner, art that speaks
to the heart, must hang on our walls.

Our extravagant coffees and desires.
Another handbag. One more pair of shoes.

A fast, sleek car; a bigger boat, bigger waves,
greater danger.

The glory of praise. May it never stop.
We are such needy beggars.

How did the pig escape the barnyard? She is free
of mud and eats from a bowl rather than a trough.

Now she sleeps, face down in her empty bowl
and perhaps it is enough, until next time.

AN EVENING WALK

Evening drifts toward darkness,
the time when dusk purples the lake
and birds tuck their songs
into the case of a wing.

The shadowed path, strewn
with wild rose petals, winds
among evergreens, the petals
delicate as Italian lace.

You could sink into silence,
deep and cool as a sheltered pool,
kneel in the sanctuary of the forest
were it not for mustard-colored snails
that inch among the petals.

You might see slime and devilish
horns, or choose to admire
the lustrous shell shaped in a perfect
spiral, eyes on graceful stems,
and the silvery trail that marks
the travels of a fascinating
creature who is always at home.

LIKE A BAD HABIT

In the beginning it was harmless.
Three starts of Virginia creeper planted
along the wall of the carriage house.
An exuberant climber, it quickly scaled
to the peak of the gable.

The following year it extended its arms
like the conductor of a grand symphony,
a boisterous celebration of rampant color,
unlimited potential.

Now the creeper has taken a turn
to the dark side. Like a bad habit,
that can be quite pleasurable,
it has become emboldened, returning
with increased force and destruction.

It has taken over, invading cracks
that permit entrance to where
it does not belong, obscuring the light
of windows, yet how can we resist
its fairy tale charm?

POETS AND RODENTS

Fluffle.

What poet could resist the word?
We gather words as if dictionaries
would soon be banned, tuck them
into the recesses of our minds,
horde them in overflowing journals.

We chew on words enjoying the crunch,
the taste, the subtle flavors, an addiction
not responsive to therapy or rehab sessions.

We are like a *gathering of wild rabbits,*
adorable creatures that were once considered
rodents: gnawing mammals with an extra set
of large incisors.

ODE TO OLD AGE

The over-ripe ear of corn still attached,
midwinter, to its spring-green stalk
may have surprised someone.

The husks, dry, grayed, and mottled with mold,
have been pulled away, the ear exposed,
the once tender kernels tough and wrinkled

and cracked. The delicate pale silk at the top
of the cob has blackened. Nostalgia
begs to remember the butter, the salt,

the picnics of an earlier season. Yet there is beauty
in the wizened features, the soft fading color,
the fierce resilience to survive the rain, the wind, and ice.

Now birds come. They have need of nourishment
as snow covers the gardens and fields and trees.
They partake and are filled.

ONE ROOM

An old abandoned schoolhouse,
the only relief as the prairie stretches
in unrelenting flatness to the horizon.

From where did the children come?
Where did they go? I can hear
their giggles. I hear them singing.

I can see their drawings of teepees
and buffalo on the walls, see
girls dressed in gingham frocks,
and suspenders hung from the thin
shoulders of boys.

I smell paste, and the biscuits and ham
in their lunch pails. Hear the school bell?
See them clambering out the door
into the wind? Into the world?

Old buildings speak with alluring voices,
holding deep mysteries inside.

The old schoolhouse is about to fall
but it tilts forward as if it feels
the thrust of lives that have moved
through that classroom and the hope
that abides in learning.

PEACEFUL VALLEY

I admire how my cousin answers the call
of restless seas, sailing to exotic places,
freedom of wind and salt air riddled
with danger, outwitting storms
and pirates who clamber aboard.

I favor a quiet life: a sunlit garden,
tranquil pools of reflection, the mercy
of days that blend into a peaceful whole.

The two of us were driving to Mt. Baker,
winding up a narrow road, when we saw it.
The road was narrow, we couldn't stop
so, we turned around and went back
and it was as if disorder had been relegated
to a distant realm.

Here a valley tucked into the foothills
of the Cascade Range, the air spiked
with the fragrance of evergreens
and mown fields. Autumn color
gentle in its arrival.

I could sink into the stillness
of this countryside. Yet I think of those
who thrive on the thrill of danger
and uncertainty—consider how
to balance the kindness of peace
with the abundance of adventure.

THE FAR EDGE OF LONGING

I keep going back to it. I don't know why
I'm so attracted to the photo of a dandelion
at its time of ripeness. Beyond the exquisite,
delicate beauty of the seed head,
there is something more.

Something about a seed partially detached
from the fragile orb, waiting for passage
to an unknown destination, the wind
an ancient conveyance.

Something about the slender shaft, the seed
poised at the tip like the point of a tiny arrow,
and the feathery fibers at the opposite end,
a miniature parachute set for descent.

Something about the potential of this humble
tuft of fluff uniquely prepared to be planted
in the place it belongs.

I imagine how it would feel to be lifted up,
carried away in the arms of the wind.
To drift in random flight, the allure
of not knowing how or when or where.

SWARM

There is a time for departure even when
there's no certain place to go.
Tennessee Williams

When it gets too crowded
they move on, and they go
together.

Worker bees stop feeding
the queen so she will be
slim enough to fly.

How do they choose who will stay
and who will go? What of those
left behind?

Bees must find a new queen
for the eroded hive and she must visit
the drone congregation for mating.

So many things to consider
for the reorganization of the hive.

I think leaving is never easy, no matter
the reason, but I'm not sure about this.

HANDOUT

Deer come daily to my door.
They talk with persuasive eyes.

I cut apples. They eat slices
from my hand. Their wildness

has marked my house
with a language of trust.

Here an easy touch,
sure to find a handout.

Aren't we all beggars?

ACKNOWLEDGMENTS

"Fragile Beauty," "Ode to Old Age," "Porcine Dreams," and "The Far Edge of Longing" appear in *Glint, MoonPath Press, 2019*

"Winter Art" appears in *The Lesson of Plums, MoonPath Press, 2020*

"The Sum of Their Work" and "Handout" appear in *Road Signs and Hobo Marks, Cyberwit, 2020*

Thanks to Dr. Karunesh Kumar Agarwal for his interest in ekphrastic poetry and for his enthusiasm to oversee the publication of this book.

Grateful thanks to Emily Gibson for generously sharing her remarkable photographs which capture moments with unique grace and light. It has been an extreme pleasure to blend my work with hers.

Thanks to Diane Stone, Sheryl Clough, and Teresa Wiley for friendship, for exploring the mysteries of the creative process, and for sharing their love of poetry with me.

And, as always, thanks to my dear friends and family—such joy!